BAC MOUNTAIN

The Light of Zen

Graham Fox

Copyright © 2016 Graham Fox

All rights reserved

CONTENTS

DEDICATION..i

DECLARATION ii

FOREWORD..iii

The Journey begins......... 1

AFTERWORD 110

THE AUTHOR 111

EXCERPT FROM: BEING KINDER TO STONES AND ROCKS..112

DEDICATION

For Julie
With flowers
In her hair.

◆◆◆

DECLARATION

You know
Right beside
The Moon
Is no moon
It's what makes
The Moon moon.

◆◆◆

FOREWORD

A fresh experience of Zen through new eyes; This book explores Zen with the explorer. It travels, not with a leader, but with the traveler discovering Zen as it goes. The book covers the ongoing journey of one follower of the way of Zen towards the light of Zen; it is written as it came, through meditation, in poetry and prose. It was not created by the author, at least not in any conventional sense, rather everything in this book happened to the author and because of this you will find a lack of order, of logical progression in the pages for which I apologize, but it is as it came. As such it is a personal journey but ultimately it is the journey of all who meditate. It is the journey of all who meditate seen, not through the eyes of a learned scholar, but through the eyes of a humble soul, an ordinary person. This is what happens, or part of it, to you and me in meditation, in Zen, following the way. To this end I hope that you will find parallels with your own journey and from this take strength. So be encouraged; remember it is not complicated, it is simple – enjoy!

Back to The Mountain was written in the early 2000s. It is followed by the Constant Arising series which runs to date. The Constant Arising series, the first volume of which is ***Being Kinder to Stones and Rocks***, will be available soon.

Graham Fox 2016

The Journey begins.........

I saw a man
Crouched
At the side
Of a pond
Staring intently
At the water

"I know
I'm in there"
He said
"I just know
I am"

I walked over
And pushed
Him in
It was the least
I could do.

◆◆◆

Going down
To the river
Dog ahead
A duckling protests
Too long
The dog returns
Duckling in mouth
Laid at my feet
All hope ends
I am the duckling
I am the dog
I duckling dog
All hope begins.

❖❖❖

ZEN THINKING

On Time

Commentary I:- we (that is us humans) are out of time, not in the sense that time has run out, but in the sense that we are outside of time. We are, if we can but allow it, outside of the illusion of time. The progression from past to present to future is in reality just a series of 'nows'. By recognizing this and thus denying time we can exist completely whole in the moment, in the now.

Commentary II:- being out of time, stepping out of time – think of time as a dimension into which pinches of timeless reality are thrown. It is a carousel and we (pinches of timeless reality) sit on the laughing horses for a brief period before time slows, the music stops and we step back into the timeless singularity that is reality.

Commentary III:- think of time as a sort of role playing game, an amusement, in which characters are spontaneously created, costumes are worn, lines are read, but in the end the curtain falls and all is one once again as it always was.

◆◆◆

There's someone
In my head
Shouting "now"
Sitting on the end
Of a needle
"Now"
Standing on my head
In Asia Minor
"Now"
Splitting a rock
With my bare hands
"Now'
Looking at the sun
Through cherry blossom
"Now Now Now."

♦♦♦

Perfection is
The allowance
Of imperfection.

♦♦♦

MOMENTS IN MEDITATION

The Tree The Grass The Cows The Gate and The Field.

In meditation I picture myself in a field. The field is bordered by a neat hedge and it is surrounded by other similar fields. In the center of the field is an oak tree but the oak tree does not thrive, it is leggy and strained. The tree is surrounded by a herd of cows that trample the grass and compress the soil starving the roots of the oxygen they need. With no root growth the tree above ground in turn does not thrive.

It strikes me that this picture is a metaphor for my mind, for *the* mind. The tree below ground, the roots, is the subconscious or the unconscious mind. It takes simple elements from the earth and uses them to nourish the tree above ground, the conscious mind. How well the tree does, how far its branches spread, how far the conscious mind reaches is a product of this nourishment. The cows represent our everyday thoughts, the thoughts that deal with the here and now, the thoughts that occupy our every waking moment. It is these cows, these thoughts, that are trampling the roots of the unconscious preventing them growing and providing the nourishment that in turn will allow the trunk and branches of the tree, of the conscious mind, to grow and spread. Now of course we need our everyday thoughts, our herd of cows, to get by in everyday life. We can't do without them yet at the same time they are stifling us, blocking out everything else. There is no time for reflection, for contemplation, for the expansion of consciousness in our everyday life. The path to realization is blocked, but what if we could live in a world where the everyday was not all pervading and this other, as yet unnamed world or reality, was allowed to grow?

How might we achieve this? Well, it is really quite simple, all we have to do is to remove the cows from the field. In other words we must let our everyday thoughts go, they must become peripheral, distant from the tree. The way to do this is simply to open the gate in the field and let the cows go, open a gate in your mind and let your thoughts go. And this, in a nutshell, is what meditation does. Without the constant trampling the roots of the tree will grow, the tree will flourish and reach out to all corners of the field connecting with every other living thing. Freeing the unconscious allows the conscious to grow and to move to another level of understanding and this other level, this unnamed world, this reality, is enlightenment. Enlightenment is the 'where' where you end up, the destination. What is it? Literally to enlighten means to shed light on, so a state of enlightenment is one in which everything is light, there are no shadows. In other words everything fits, the many disparate things of this world become one. And this, in a nutshell, is the aim of Zen.

It is in this way that we can become one mind that is to say connected to and part of the whole. This one mind can also be thought of as 'no mind', no individual mind. Think of lily pads; single leaves floating on the pond (you and me) but underneath the water the stems join to the same root and that root is bound to the earth which in turn is bound to everything else. In this way everything is one and 'no mind' is achieved. It should however be noted that we are not putting things back together here, everything always was and always will be one, we are merely coming to that understanding, and this coming realization, in a nutshell, is the path of Zen. And so that is all about the tree, the grass, the cows, the gate and the field.

❖❖❖

> Looking in the water
> Of the old pond
> I see Buddha
> Washing his face
> A water-boatman
> Slides by.

❖❖❖

MOMENTS IN MEDITATION

The bath mat I sit on for comfort when meditating in time becomes the sacred prayer mat.

The shower cubicle I sit in because it is the quietest place in the house becomes a confessional.

My notebook for writing meditational musings becomes the holy prayer book.

The scented candle I light for atmosphere becomes the light of the Holy Spirit.

Things I say to myself in meditation to still the mind become incantations in the holy ritual.

The bell that rings to stir me from meditation becomes the bell that summons the faithful.

So it goes, the mundane and functional things of inner contemplation become the rituals and icons of religions in time. Of themselves they are harmless as long as it is clear that they have no meaning. To give these things meaning, to give them weight, is like putting clothes on an elephant, it is pointless and in fact hinders your view of the elephant. Beware the icon, beware rituals.

♦♦♦

On The Road to (Basho's Poem).

Coming to
Old pond
It's frozen.

Comment:- *Basho was a famous wandering Zen poet. Perhaps his most famous poem was,*

Old pond
Slip splash
A frog.

♦♦♦

ZEN THINKING

Linear Thinking (Trapped in a Two-Dimensional World).

Man takes to a path from the point of birth and even before it could be argued, it is a consequence of being. The man in our story is no exception as indeed there can't be any. But enough of this, our fellow is following a path which cuts a thin almost imperceptible line across the great plain. The path itself is not difficult, but it can be easy to lose, easy to mistake. Occasionally along the way our fellow is helped by signs, confirmations, that the path is right. We join him now at one such confirmation.

An old man sits at a point where the path is crossed by many other paths. Pointing straight ahead our fellow asks, "Is this the way?"
"Yes yes," the old man says, waving rather impatiently before returning to whatever it is that he is doing sat alone in the middle of nowhere.

Our fellow therefore continues on his way, bolstered by this confirmation. Presently he ascends a small rise which, strangely enough, is quite common in the flat and featureless plain if you go far enough. At the top of this rise our fellow notices a change. He stops in his tracks. He is no longer alone with the endless plain, it now has an end. In the distance a mountain range stretches across his path as far as he can see in either direction. There is nothing in between and the path leads, as far as he can see, directly to the mountains. My path may be faint he thinks but it is clear, I must to the mountains and then I must cross. And with this our fellow sets off with renewed vigor. Many days and nights pass and all the while the path is straight and true and all the while the mountains in the distance slowly grow. The time finally comes when the mountains are no longer in the distance; they are right in front of him, above him even. His trusty path does not let him down; he can see that it winds up the side of the mountain to a pass. At last he thinks, this is it and with that he makes for the pass. The pass is steep and narrow and the walls are sheer but our fellow perseveres until he is stopped in his tracks; a huge rock fall has blocked the pass. There is no way round, over or through. Our good fellow is stumped and he sits facing the rock not knowing what to do. Presently he heaves a long sigh realizing that there is only one thing that he can do. Picking himself up he turns back down the mountain heading for the crossroads many days away. Clearly, he thinks, this is not the way, at least not any more; one of the other paths must be the way.

Many days later our fellow finds himself back at the crossroads. The old man is still there still doing whatever he is doing in the middle of nowhere.
"That path is not the way," our fellow says to the old man, trying to contain his exasperation, "Is one of these other paths the way?" he continues.
"Yes, yes," says the old man.
"Well which one?" says our fellow, now passing exasperation and entering annoyance.
"Yes, yes, all of them," says the old man waving his arms in a circle. Now it is the turn of our fellow to wave his arms. He throws them up to the sky.

"Does it matter which one I take?" he says.

"No," the old man replies.

"And will I end up having to come back here whichever one I take?" our fellow asks, a dawn of realization coming into his mind.

"Most likely," says the old man.

"And you, what are you doing?" says our fellow.

"Oh! I am on the path like you," says the old man.

"Now I think I understand," says our fellow and with that he sits down beside the old man.

And so our story ends with our fellow sat right where he is, where he has always been, where he will always be.

❖❖❖

It was in that gap
Between the beginning
Of a step
And the ending
Between leaving the ground
And returning

Something – undefined
Formed and then
Unformed
An eternity in waiting
When finally it formed
It had – no form

The linear progress
Made by the step
Remains
The only evidence
Of change
And yet it is only that
Which was formed
That is – of consequence.

♦♦♦

Last flower
Also first.

♦♦♦

Flesh and mind
Dissolve
Bones to ash
A breeze
Blows.

♦♦♦

MOMENTS IN MEDITATION

The definition of the great Zen quest is to rejoin the undefined, the undefinable, by not defining, by not being defined. It is to that sea that this drop returns.

♦♦♦

Pictures from
Another room
I have seen.

♦♦♦

On water
That supports
No hell
Is reflected
The last face
To the Sun.

Comment:- *'water that supports no hell' is Buddha nature. 'The last face to the sun' is at the back of the mirror, it is behind everything, it reflects the Sun, it is the light of the Sun, it is enlightenment.*

♦♦♦

Art
Touches.

♦♦♦

MOMENTS IN MEDITATION

In the Zen quest it is required to fish without a line or a net, the water must not be disturbed and under no circumstances must a fish be caught.
Sounds easy – doesn't it?

♦♦♦

Purple clouds
Pelicans
Pass through.

♦♦♦

Water
On my head
I am the rain.

♦♦♦

Shoes
Not worn
Are worn.

♦♦♦

MOMENTS IN MEDITATION

I used to think everything had a name, I just didn't know them all, but then I found things with no name and slowly I came to realize that nothing really has a name. No thing is named. There are no names.

♦♦♦

Sailing into
The storm
Under
A darkened sun
Mindful of
The scent
Of jasmine.

♦♦♦

Fearsome fire
Breathing dragon
Fly for one day.

♦♦♦

Wind
On water
Moon
No moon.

♦♦♦

MOMENTS IN MEDITATION

What does it mean in Zen when, in answer to a deep and heart felt question, your teacher simply replies, "A blade of grass" or says nothing at all but just points? It means forget the question, to question is irrelevant.

♦♦♦

Questions
Of fabric
Of function
Bash
My head
This is.

♦♦♦

If you sit
Long enough
The walls
Will crumble
Apple crumble?
-Yes please.

♦♦♦

ZEN THINKING

Zen thinking is not complex; it is not obscure. Zen thinking is simple, stupid simple, so simple it goes unnoticed. Zen thinking is essentially not thinking.

❖❖❖

In Zen
The mundane
Is most
Extra-ordinary.

❖❖❖

Sermons
From an
Empty chair
Bow
My head.

❖❖❖

ZEN THINKING

Understanding that a grain of sand is the beach and the beach a grain of sand; the robin is both singing and not singing. Time and space cut through.

> Time and space
> Cut through
> Walnut writes
> A symphony.

◆◆◆

> There are
> No
> Empty chairs
> In
> Empty rooms.

◆◆◆

MOMENTS IN MEDITATION

It takes no time to travel between nowhere and somewhere or indeed the reverse. There is also no distance involved. This is simply because time and space do not in reality exist. Nowhere and somewhere, here and there, now and then are all the same. They can simply be summarized as 'here and now,' that is all there is; the rest is an illusion.

◆◆◆

On Basho's Poem.

Old pond
Slip splash
A human.

❖❖❖

Perfect edges
Meeting
Disappearing
Jigsaw
One picture.

❖❖❖

MOMENTS IN MEDITATION

A young man came across a much older man at the beach. He was sitting all alone cross-legged with a bowl of water and a brush. The young man watched him as he picked up a pebble, dipped it in the water and then scrubbed it with the brush, before placing it back on the beach. He continued watching for some time before, against his better judgment, he let curiosity reign and asked, "What are you doing?" The old man replied, "Washing pebbles." I knew it thought the young man, ask a silly question…. then he thought of a clever retort, "But the waves already do that," he said.
"Precisely," said the old man.

Comment:-

*What play is here
What a perfect peach
Washing pebbles
On a beach.*

◆◆◆

The Naming of Birds.

Crying and laughing
On cherry-blossom
Wetted pavements
I let go.

Comment:- *no thing actually has a name.*

◆◆◆

MOMENTS IN MEDITATION

Peace has nothing to do with fighting or not fighting.
Peace is a state of mind. Fighting and not fighting are
states of being.

◆◆◆

MOMENTS IN MEDITATION

Zen (the road to) is learning to walk through walls that are not there.

❖❖❖

The displacement of
A water-boat-man
Hardly bends
Light still lighter
The Zen mind.

❖❖❖

No flag stirs
The Zen mind.

Comment:- *this poem references the stillness of the Zen mind, its lack of worldly allegiance and of course the story of the two monks discussing what makes a flag wave, none of which really matters, just look straight through. Two lines, two statements, like pillars they stand.*

❖❖❖

ZEN THINKING

Zen mind takes no space, it has a displacement of zero.

Zen mind does not change with time, unaffected by time it is timeless.

Zen mind is still, because it is non relative and all movement is necessarily relative.

♦♦♦

On Basho's Poem

Old pond
Reflection
Beyond stars.

♦♦♦

All that is said
All that is done
Does not disturb.

♦♦♦

ZEN THINKING

In the physical world stillness does not exist. From planets hurtling through macro-space to strings vibrating in subatomic space everything is in motion relative to everything else.
In the Zen world movement does not exist; there is only stillness. This is because Zen is One and all movement is relative, which requires two; a thing and a something to go past that thing, Zen just doesn't have that.

❖❖❖

Nothing
Is quintessential
It is
Quintessentially
Nothing.

❖❖❖

On Basho's Poem (*irreverently*)

Blank page
Ink splash
A poem.

❖❖❖

ZEN THINKING

Some examples of oppositional words;

movement – stillness
presence – absence
here – there
then – now
matter – antimatter
clockwise – anticlockwise.

None of these words are oppositional in Zen.

♦♦♦

Doggy Dharma

Desperate kind sad
Dull fierce loyal
Loving
Eyes
Nose ears and tail
Paws.

♦♦♦

Contradictions:
Logic with
The steps
Removed.

◆◆◆

ZEN THINKING

There is 'thinking outside the box' there is 'blue sky thinking' and then there is Zen thinking. Zen thinking is thinking without reference, feeling if you like. This is not emotional feeling though; it is more like feeling in the dark with the fingers of your mind. Things are discovered (explored) as they *are* in Zen thinking, not as they are 'relative to' or 'by their interaction with' but *de novo*. In fact the phrase *de novo* meaning 'as new' or 'from the beginning' pretty much encapsulates Zen thinking.

◆◆◆

No ink
No paper
No words
Just *this*.

◆◆◆

Names – places – times
Swallowed
In the void
Listen.

♦♦♦

If
You understand
Nothing else
Understand *this*.

♦♦♦

MOMENTS IN MEDITATION

It is a small wooden hut set on earthen ground with a small stone hearth, a cot, a rough wooden table and a desk and chair. On the table is a pitcher of water and a stack of bowls and pans; some vegetables wait with a knife beside. The hearth is piled with logs waiting to be lit. The cot is made with a simple blanket. Under the single window sits a desk with drawer open and chair withdrawn. Papers are strewn on the desk along with brushes of various sizes and a pen; a pot of ink stands in the corner next to a burned candle. From the window can be seen a small stream bubbling through a wood and in the distance a snow-capped mountain joins the sky. The hut is empty. Who lives here?

♦♦♦

A small part of me
The first drop
Wants to go home
Now it is raining
Buddha wash my face.

•••

Absorb
Become
Reflect
Disappear.

•••

On the great
Unburnished plain
Sits the grasshopper.

Comment:- *on the great dusty plain of our relative thinking sits the grasshopper, staring us in the face, in need of no words, beyond the relative, just sitting, representing (whisper it quietly) the absolute.*

•••

MOMENTS IN MEDITATION

Just as the fastest horse does not know he is the fastest, so the enlightened man cannot know he is enlightened. Speed of course is relative, now the horse is not capable of making comparison and to know you are the fastest you

have to be able to compare, *ergo* the horse cannot know
that he is the fastest. In the case of the enlightened man,
the state of enlightenment is absolute, it just is, it is not
relative to something else, certainly not non-enlightenment
despite what its name implies (it is
after all only a name). So, in this case, although the man
understands relativity and is able to make comparison, the
state of enlightenment will not bear it; admitting
enlightenment admits not-enlightenment thus creating a
dichotomy, a relativity, which cannot exist in
enlightenment, thus the man who says or knows he is
enlightened cannot be. The outcome, for both horse and
man thankfully is the same; neither have a clue what is
going on but you can be sure that the enlightened man will
bet on the fastest horse.

> The fastest horse
> Does not know
> The enlightened man
> Does not know
> Write me fifty pages
> Write me one word.

♦♦♦

> You know
> Right beside
> The Moon
> There is
> No moon
> It's what makes
> The Moon moon.

MOMENTS IN MEDITATION

The only thing in this existence that is not real, oddly enough, is you and me. Animals are real, trees and rocks are real, the ocean is real and the Sun and the Moon and the stars and the sky, all real, but we, we are not. We exist in a state of delusion not in reality. The journey we must take is not to some other place, we have already done that, but it is from that other place (delusion) back to reality. The journey is not from here to there but rather from there (delusion) back to here (reality) and it is really just one step. The journey is *back* to reality because we were born in reality but grew into delusion. The journey is in fact a coming home. This is the journey of Zen.

❖❖❖

Building the imaginable
On the unimaginable
That is what you
You and I do
Well my friend
Empty your pockets
And open the door
Meet the unimaginable
Chrysanthemum frog.

❖❖❖

Let everything go
Let your mind relax
And stick your head
In three pounds of flax.

Comment:- *a monk asked Tozan, "what is Buddha?" He replied, "three pounds of flax." (a well known Buddhist Q&A).*

◆◆◆

MOMENTS IN MEDITATION

The dharma is not to be learned or followed; it is to be waited for, to be met. The dharma is met through meditation where it is simply entered then, like a mighty river, it takes you.

◆◆◆

Pouring water
On to
Concrete floor.

Comment:- *nothing to say about this poem. I almost didn't include it but looking at it I could not not.*

◆◆◆

I am fog
I am mist
I am air
Catch me
Catch me
Like a cold
Not
Like a bird
Catch me
But
Don't catch me.

❖❖❖

A life spent looking
Looking for tomorrow
Is wasted
It is tomorrow.

❖❖❖

Zen
Is simple
It is
Being simple
It is
Simply being.

Comment:- *not easy!*

❖❖❖

ZEN THINKING

Enlightenment is a state beyond state. It cannot be stamped, filed, categorized or even referred to. It is no state, boundless, beyond and yet it is where we are.

♦♦♦

Demand nothing less
From yourself
Than a full apology.

♦♦♦

In my mind
I met a man
With a mind
So clear and
So pure
That he had
No answers
Because of this
All the questions
Disappeared.

♦♦♦

Walk
Like a child
Blue-eyed
Pigment less
See and
Be seen

❖❖❖

Waves come
To wash pebbles
On the beach
Fabulously.

❖❖❖

ZEN THINKING

People say infinity is vast but when a flower grows there are an infinite number of possibilities. One flower fills infinity so infinity is small then. Now where did I put that flower, it is here somewhere, it must be. I should hold it up in the air *(somebody already did that)*

One flower
Fills infinity.

❖❖❖

Beyond explanation
Beyond logic
Into nonsense
And beyond nonsense
Into no sense
And beyond no sense
And beyond beyond
Until finally a clearing
Turn and blow
All the trees
Fall down.

Comment:- *beyond beyond is back again but you have to go.*

♦♦♦

MOMENTS IN MEDITATION

How big is a Mosquito?

As you sit to begin meditation you see a mosquito sitting beside you, if indeed they do sit. What do you do? You know it will surely bite you but, as yet, it has not. Do you squash it, remove its life, effectively try it, sentence it and carry out the sentence before it has even committed a crime? At this moment despite your suspicions of a conspiracy before the fact, you have to admit that the mosquito is actually innocent; even if he were guilty, do you have the right to remove his life? After all the mosquito is only being a mosquito; it has Buddha nature, it cannot not have Buddha nature, so, kill Buddha nature?

On the one hand life is a practical everyday thing which necessarily turns, like a wheel, to death and back to life again; life carries within it the seed of death. So, turn he wheel? On the other hand life is precious and should be preserved wherever possible. Should you turn the wheel when you don't really have to?

So now: enter meditation with a live mosquito and be troubled by its presence, or kill the mosquito, enter meditation and be troubled by its absence? Whatever you choose to do, there is a certainty here: you have either killed that mosquito or you have not, in any case ask yourself, how big was that mosquito? This I say,

> "No questions
> No answers
> You and
> The mosquito
> For eternity."

❖❖❖

Getting to the Other Side (of the River).

> Just walk
> To the end
> The thin end
> Not the fat end
> And both sides
> Will become same.

❖❖❖

ZEN THINKING

All Zen writing is just words you know
What do these words tell us?
They tell us to think
Think beyond words.

♦♦♦

Kicking stones
In the Zen garden
I see
A cat has crapped
In the sand.

♦♦♦

I am an idiot
Waiting to happen.

♦♦♦

Open Eye - Closed Eye Suite

Master,
"A face, one eye open, one eye closed, which eye sees?"

Pupil,
"The open eye."

Master,
"Yes, of course, the open eye but the closed eye also sees.
There is never not seeing, no such thing exists."

One eye open
One eye closed
Ready for all
Scent of jasmine.

Eyes open
Eyes closed
Moon
No moon.

◆◆◆

MOMENTS IN MEDITATION

A young monk is exploring in the mountains when he comes across a cave; he enters. At first it is too dark and he cannot find the way. He thinks of giving up but the thought of somewhere new, somewhere unexplored, spurs him on. Gradually his eyes adjust and he finds a little stream emerging from deep in the cave. He reasons that the stream must have come from somewhere and that somewhere, that origin, that beginning, is where he wants to be and so he follows it upstream. At first the way is easy but it gets darker and darker and tighter and tighter. Now the way is difficult, the stream is very small, he can no longer see it and the tinkling sound it makes bounces off the rock all around confusing him giving him no direction. So he goes by feel alone following the tiny trickle with his fingers. Soon however the way becomes too tight and the young man cannot pass. Still feeling the water as it disappears into the rock he reasons to himself that if something as simple as water can find a way, can pass, then surely he, with all his training, should be able to do likewise. And it is here, deep underground, inside a rock, that he has his moment, his satori, the flash of light, of insight, that shows him the way. The water passes precisely because it is simple, fluid, formless. He does not pass because he is not simple, he is complex, he is not fluid, he holds on to form. Clearly he must become water. He must be simple, fluid, transparent, formless, able to pass anywhere, reflecting all and yet allowing all to pass through him.

And so, for this monk there is no need to go further in the

cave; he has found his way. So it is with all who seek. The objective is not a place, physical point or state but the way; the way is the goal. On his return to the monastery the young monk wrote these words,
"Water passes and leaves no trace yet it sustains and nourishes; so shall I be."

>>>Dissolving
Into water
I am free.

♦♦♦

Chasing feathers in
The monastery kitchen
Sunlight plays on
The stone flag floor
No duck is dead

♦♦♦

Zen is
The empty Jesus
A mist
Dissolving.

♦♦♦

MOMENTS IN MEDITATION

The rope tightens and 'pings' as fibers tear. It frays and finally breaks. The bonds between things come apart. This is the Zen way and it allows things to be experienced not in context, not out of context but in no context. And so for example we consider a cat drinking milk from a bowl. Now, with bonds broken, there is only 'cat', 'milk' and 'bowl', all floating free. The three come together and are parted. The only change is that the milk is now inside the cat (at some time it was presumably inside a bottle and before that, a cow). What happens is the same, how you see it is different and this makes all the difference.

❖❖❖

No other Eden
No promised land
No new tomorrow
This earth
At my feet
This *this*
Now

Now
I grind my head
In the ground
Now
I kiss the soil
Now
A donkey
Steps on me.

❖❖❖

Watching someone
Walking straight
Into a plate
Glass window
Is funny
Doing it
Is not
Fish gasping
On the ground
Also not.

Comment:- *nobody is laughing, especially not the fish although it may look like it.*

❖❖❖

MOMENTS IN MEDITATION

Analyzing this and analyzing that is a dead-end way in Zen because it always produces a result, an 'other', which then itself must be analyzed. This is a mental maze with no exit. The true way is that of water. Flow over through and in everything. Do not divide, encompass, then you will see that a horse is a flower and a horse is just a horse.

❖❖❖

When all the castles
Are turned to sand
And the sun melts
On the horizon
Finally I will be
The ocean so
Take me down
Take me down
To the water.

◆◆◆

MOMENTS IN MEDITATION

Originally everything was ONE. There was no need for names, differences, comparisons; everything was ONE and ONE was 'same'. This in effect was paradise and paradise was a constant; it was *the* constant. Here there was no need for words to describe 'same' and, as paradise was a constant, no need for time, no need for space. But paradise, oneness, was lost, it was shattered into a trillion pieces and we (mankind) did it. So, welcome to 'paradise lost', our invention, but the ONE has not gone, there can be 'paradise found' and this is the journey that Zen makes.

◆◆◆

The Sandals The Monastery The Pond and The Frog (and A Cricket).

A pair of sandals
Old worn and torn
Sitting on a stone flag
Outside the monastery
A cricket lands lightly
On the leather strap
Monastery collapses

A pair of sandals
Old worn and torn
Sitting on the grass
Beside the pond
A frog jumps in
Sandals belong
To frog

Light a candle
On the grass
Beside the pond
It is a monastery
Blow it out
Frog swallows monastery
Pick up the sandals
Walk away.

Comment;- *so how should I paint this? Brushes ink and paper ready; start with the monastery and the pond then maybe the sandals and the candle? – no? Perhaps I'll just do a little frog and leave it at that, the rest is kind of implied anyway.*

MOMENTS IN MEDITATION

The Man Who Knew Too Many Things.

I knew a man, many years ago, who knew many many things. He would spend his days telling them to people, edifying them; this made him happy.
I met the same man many years later and he knew only one thing. He would spend his days telling this one thing, only this, to people and this made him very happy.
I met the same man recently and, do you know, he'd forgotten everything, all the many many things, even the one thing. The funny thing is that this made him even happier, of course he didn't know that, how could he, he'd forgotten everything, but I could see it.

Comment:- *knowing and not knowing, happy to not know; our fellow read all the books, distilled them to a fine liquor, bottled it, put it on the shelf and forgot about it. I was going to say something here about the scent of jasmine or frogs but I've forgotten!*

♦♦♦

How to say without
Becoming attached
To words to sound
It's simple
Don't say listen
To silence.

Comment:- *it may be simple but it is not easy. The process of becoming non-attached can be itself attachment. The following poem sums it up:*

> Let it go
> Then let
> Letting it go
> Go
> Then just go
> Finish terminate end stop
> Right…………..good
> Silence
> A mouse farts!

◆◆◆

MOMENTS IN MEDITATION

The Man Who Kept Birds

I knew a man once who had a beautiful carved wooden aviary in which he kept many birds; these were beautiful birds, prizewinning birds. Now this man was very proud of his birds and they made him happy but also he felt just a little bit guilty. Why so? Well because, despite all arguments that these birds were bred for captivity and would not survive in the wild, he felt they should still be free. Every day this feeling and the associated guilt grew a little and the beautiful wooden door to the beautiful wooden aviary became more difficult to close. He began to feel not like a helper, a friend to the birds, but like an owner, a possessor and dare he think it, a jailer; the birds were not singing 'I love you' but 'please release me'.

Eventually his wife, Magda, noticed his growing restlessness and asked what it could possibly be that had upset him so. When he told her she laughed and said that the problem was simple with a simple solution, "You cannot carry the fate of all of these birds," she said. "It is too heavy. You must go and talk to the leader of the birds and do a deal with him. Now you love your birds and would not be without at least one so offer them all their freedom, save one, your favorite, and he is to give you his fate freely in exchange for the freedom of the rest."

The man liked this solution, he liked it very much and so he went to talk to the birds. A deal was struck and he picked his favorite. He then opened the beautiful wooden door to the beautiful wooden aviary, his favorite stayed and all the other birds flew away. Now the man and his bird quickly settled down and were very happy, so happy that he built the bird a gilded cage that was the talk of the town and he made sure that the bird wanted for nothing. Every day he would go to the bird, the bird would come out and sit on his shoulder and sing and he would feed it grapes and sunflower seeds until it would eat no more. Never once did they have a cross word and never once did he have to close the cage door as the bird would not fly away. He was very happy and the bird seemed very happy what with all that singing. He was very happy that is until one day. One day he asked the bird what he sung about. "Oh! Not much," said the bird. "Just trees and rivers, the mountains, sky, spring migration, that sort of thing."

From that day the man began to feel a familiar feeling and it grew and grew until, in his mind, he was the guiltiest man in all the valley. The fate of this bird, although given to him freely was still too heavy to carry and he knew he would have to do something about it. So he went and talked to the bird, "You have given your freedom to me in exchange for the freedom of others," he said. "Now I realize that the pact we made was not just; a man can carry only one freedom, his own, any other is too heavy, so I give it back to you." Then the bird whispered something in his ear and the man nodded and smiled. The next day the man went to the bird and, putting it on his shoulder, set about the gilded cage. He spent all day cutting and shaping the gilded bars of the gilded cage until he had made a gilded tree. He set the gilded tree in his garden and from it he hung many fruits and bags of seeds and nuts. Then he set the bird in the tree and the bird began to sing and he waited. Presently other birds came and they began to sing and this brought more birds until his tree was full. His bird was now just one of the many that came and went to the tree as they pleased. The man visited his tree every day from then on and sometimes the birds were there and sometimes they were not and this made the man very very happy.

> This man
> He built a cage
> Around his heart
> A songbird came
> And tore it apart.

♦♦♦

Matter
Does not
Matter
Nothing
Matters.

Comment:- *substance has no real substance and no substance has real substance; so we go into the pot melting.*

❖❖❖

The sun has seven sides
It's a seven sided sun
This you just have to know

The hippopotamus is
A seven sided sun.

Comment:- *here we talk of the interchangeability of matter (form) which does matter.*

❖❖❖

Zen mind
Is very big
It would take
Heavy equipment
To move it or
Just a breeze.

❖❖❖

> Talking to Buddha
> Is just
> Teasing the fat boy
> And the ears
> Don't get me started!

◆◆◆

MOMENTS IN MEDITATION

A student went to see a great master and asked to be taught. The master agreed, asked him to sit and gave him a candy. The student bowed and put it in his pocket.
"This is wrong," said the master. "Go, come back tomorrow."
So the student, somewhat confused, left. He came back the next morning and once again the master told him to sit. The master then left and only came back in the evening. He gave the student a candy. The student, very hungry by now, unwrapped it, threw away the wrapping, and ate the candy. The master smiled and said,
"This is right; before we were both wrong, now we are both right. The lesson is over, you can go."
What does this little tale tell?

> Take only this
> When needed
> Give only this
> When needed.

◆◆◆

The sound of geese
Leaving
Almost too painful

The sound of geese
Arriving
Almost too painful.

Comment:- *I can't, I'm in too much pain!*

♦♦♦

Hairs
On the stems
Of gooseberries
Hold up the stars.

♦♦♦

MOMENTS IN MEDITATION

I met a man on a beach scratching a poem on a pebble.
"Why not write on paper," I said.
"People burn paper," he said. With that he stood up and hurled the pebble into the sea. His poem?

Nothing
Is
Permanent.

I wonder how many poems there are on pebbles under the sea.

◆◆◆

When jasmine
Flowers
The scent
Of jasmine.

◆◆◆

To a reason
Beyond reason
Beyond even
Mad hatters
Where everything
Describes one
And one
Describes every thing
And then
Beyond description
To where words fall
Into alphabet soup
Then, *this* then
Please
Pass the spoon.

♦♦♦

MOMENTS IN MEDITATION

Master to pupil,
"Show your understanding."

Pupil to master,
"When two things are touching they are called 'together' when really the space between them is infinite."

Master,
"This is good but you are still a child playing with toys, try again."
The pupil bows, goes away and comes back the next day with,
"The brackets on my wall have no screws yet the shelf stays up."

Master,
"This is the same, try again."
The pupil bows, goes away and comes back, this time several days later with,
"Where are you now?"

Master,
"No, no, this is same. 'Things together', 'shelf,' brackets', 'where', 'you' – all same. You must throw your toys away."
The pupil bows, goes away and this time he is gone for a long time. Eventually he returns and sits in front of his master. He says nothing. From his pockets he produces three eggs placing them on the mat in front of him. The first egg he smashes with his fist. The second egg he eats. The third egg he holds up and then throws out of the

window. The pupil bows his head.

Master,
"Ha! Ha! Good but where is the fourth egg?

Smash mountain
Eat rocks
Shit mountain
Walk on mountain.

One two three, FOUR eggs – yes!"
Master bows.
Pupil bows.

♦♦♦

Banana Split Suite

Welcome
To the end
Of thinking…

…I am a banana…

…But I am not
A payphone
In Seattle…

…There now
I think
It's stopped…
…………….

Welcome
To the end
Of thinking
Yes but
Which end?
Actually
It doesn't matter
You mean
All that effort…
Yep! 'fraid so
By the way
I am a ban-
Yes! I know.

❖❖❖

MOMENTS IN MEDITATION

A Zen master gives an introductory lecture to new students every year; it is boring and complicated. One year he thinks to himself,
"Why do I give this boring and complicated lecture, Zen is not boring, Zen is not complicated. So he decides to change things and when time comes for the lecture he greets the students and says,
"This year I am not going to regale you with the history of Zen, its terms, its rituals, all of this you will learn, or not, in due course. No, this year I am simply going to show you what we do here." And with that he clicks a button and the first slide appears. It is a picture of a room, shuttered and cluttered with all manner of things, all useful in their own way, but all tripping over each other (actually it is his own room).

"This is the room you are in right now," he says. A few students giggle because clearly this is not the room they are in right now. The master clicks again and the second slide appears. It is a picture of another room. This room is empty, the walls are white and the windows are open.

"This is the room we are going to show you," he says. There is more amusement among the students; "No chance to make coffee then," one says. The master clicks again and a third slide appears. It is a picture of a room, cluttered and shuttered.

"And this is the room you will end up in," he says. No laughter this time; after a pause someone pipes up,
"But isn't that the first room, the one we are supposed to be in right now?"

"Precisely," says the master. "You have it! Enjoy your

studies," and with that he was gone; out of the door in a swirl of robes.

"I think that went well," he said to himself, "Nice and simple." Behind him the class just looked at each other. "Perhaps there is a secret code in the pictures," someone said.

"I don't think so," several people said.

Comment:- *something here is left unsaid; when you return to the first room take the second room with you. The second room is the first room.*

❖❖❖

Empty sandals
At Buddha's feet
Bang the ground
What does *this* mean?
Buddha laughs.

Comment:- *sandals are here symbols of attachment to the ground, to man's ways. Empty sandals mean release, freedom, enlightenment if you like which, in this case means that the writer should know what 'this' means and this is why Buddha laughs.*

❖❖❖

So many words
For snow
Buddha is still
Laughing.

❖❖

MOMENTS IN MEDITATION

Pupil,
"How do you know what is behind you?"

Master,
"Everything in front of me is a mirror."

Pupil,
"What if there is a mirror behind you?"

Master,
"Precisely."

♦♦♦

Grit
In my shoe
The cat barks
Next time
Boulders.

Comment: - *then what will cat do?*

♦♦♦

ZEN THINKING

Transmission in the mechanical world typically involves a series of metal rods, linkages or pivots and cogs which transmit energy from point A to point B. there is much noise, much grinding of metal, much heat generated and hence much wastage of energy.

Transmission in the religious or spiritual world is via the word. Words transmit the energy of understanding from person A to person B. Here also there is much noise, much grinding of words, much heat generated and hence much energy lost.

In both worlds it is true that the fewer the components used to transmit energy the less the loss of energy is. This is why we have engineers. It is also why we have poets and why we have the Haiku, the shortest form of all poetry, virtually no wastage, almost 100% transmission – why not try one today!

❖❖❖

Zen is not taught
Zen is revealed
Everything already
In place.

❖❖❖

I breathe
And
The stone
Beside me
Breathes.

Comment:- *the rock's breathing is not separated from my breathing. Moreover on a larger scale we are not talking here about billions of entities breathing on one planet but 'one breathing' everywhere, not billions of Buddha natures on Earth but one Buddha nature throughout. The poem describes one event.*

•••

ZEN THINKING

The bull and the bullfighter, where is Zen nature here? Dr. Suzuki has it with the bullfighter, R. H. Blythe says that it is surely with the bull. If you say Zen nature is with the bullfighter you are wrong. If you say Zen nature is with the bull you are wrong. The two are opposites, metaphorically and physically, and Zen is not concerned with opposites, with right and wrong, so, a new answer; Zen weaves these two together and blows them apart in bloody conflict but it picks no side, Suzuki and Blythe have left Zen in the dirt.

Now consider this;

for the bullfighter take away the bull and he is just a man in fancy dress, for the bull take away the bullfighter and he is just a cow with horns. Now the question is undressed we see that it has no grounding, no substance, it is a trick question asking us to judge man and bull by the roles given to them.

The bullfighter
And the bull
Stand alone
The crowd
Has gone home
"Let's end
This silly play
Lets walk away"
A fly lands
On the bull's-eye.

❖❖❖

Constant
Arising.

Comment:- *this is the Zen universe (the shortest word picture of same).*

❖❖❖

ZEN THINKING

'The floor is dirty because the dog walked mud in.'

The floor *is*, there *is* the dog and there *is* mud.

Now, analyzing these two statements we can see in the first the causal linkage between the elements. Assumptions are made which, however likely, are fundamentally wrong, too much weight is put on the shoulders of things, too much burden. Reading between the lines of this statement, it is telling us that mud is a dirty thing and by association the dog is dirty, the floor is innocent in all of this and has only become dirty through the fault of the mud (for existing) and the dog (for walking).

The second statement merely lists the protagonists it does not ascribe blame and it does not rule in or out any possible eventualities.

Here we see how a simple statement can put a loaded gun in your hand and pull the trigger. Perhaps if we were all to rearrange our sentences, our thinking, to encompass just what *is* and not what we assume, everything would be a little easier to love.

♦♦♦

On a beach
Of perfect pebbles
Which one
Do I throw
Into the ocean?
None silly!
The perfect ocean
Will come up
And pick
One itself.

Comment:- *throw yourself in why don't you!*

♦♦♦

Zen is simply
Being awake
Simply.

❖❖❖

MOMENTS IN MEDITATION

Zen, that stealthy intruder creeps into your house. It eats candlesticks and changes written words then it plays mouse to your cat and, like Jerry, always gets away.

❖❖❖

Important
In Haiku
Not to
Waste words
Dogblancmangepoo
Oops!
I've spilt some.

❖❖❖

And in
The very very
Long grass
Yes
Oh! Yes it is
A tiger
And it will
Kill you

In Zen
That tiger
Is a teapot
But still
It will
Kill you

So I want
You to say
Twenty times
A day
"I am a teapot"
Chocolate one
Of course
A real one
Would be far
Too dangerous.

♦♦♦

ZEN THINKING

When you breathe the space between breaths is not breathing; so it is with trees, in fact anything, the space next to a tree is 'not tree'.
These two could be viewed as exemplars of 'form' and 'no form'. Form only exists in that there is 'no form' to show it and 'no form' only exists in that it is shown by 'form'. The two are intertwined and when we unwind them we find them to be just one. Form is 'no form' and 'no form' is 'form'.

❖❖❖

If I had a parrot (called Bobo)
And I was not aware of flight
And I swam from here to Hawaii
And when I got there I met Bobo
I would think Bobo could swim.

Comment:- *maybe Bobo is a fish – a parrot fish – ha ha!*

❖❖❖

ZEN THINKING

Falling into the water is a relief after so much effort balancing on a surf board. Even falling into the air is a release after spending so much time clinging to the mountain, though the consequences may be dire.
This relief, this release, comes with the ending of the pretense of balancing, clinging, holding on. And when you let go, when you fall, you fall into Zen; what you fell from quickly becomes irrelevant.

After all
The clinging
After all
The balancing
When you
Let go
Of everything
Finally there
Is Zen.

❖❖❖

Through the eye
Of a needle
Reflecting
Perfect heaven
Sits
The fat boy.

❖❖❖

Looking at the sky
Sandhill Cranes
Having flown by.

❖❖❖

ZEN THINKING

When confronted by something, when given something, do not take it piece by piece, individual pieces have no meaning, take the whole. A piece does not tell you the picture of the puzzle.

A box of frogs
Is
A box of frogs
It is not
Many individual frogs
And a box

Do not bring me
One frog
Bring me
The box.

❖❖❖

Sweeping the floor
Makes the sound
Of strings
Somewhere
A dog barks
The whole
New York
Philharmonic
Orchestra
Resigns.

◆◆◆

ZEN THINKING

Why is Zen so invested in 'something' and 'nothing'? It is because these two, so called, opposites neatly encompass the falsehood of our thinking. If we break the edges between 'thing' and 'no thing', deny this border, then we can free our minds, our thinking. It is only in this state that we can admit Zen.

◆◆◆

No thing
Exists
Without
Nothing.

◆◆◆

Balancing an apple
On top
Of an olive
Is easier
Inside your stomach.

Comment:- *break it down man, break it down!*

♦♦♦

ZEN THINKING

Just as the border between countries is an imaginary line so the border between 'thing' and 'no thing', substance and no substance, is imaginary. The one is part of and at the same time defines the other. This is why we say 'form is no form' and 'no form is form'. This understanding is fundamental not just intellectual. It must be felt, it must be expected, in the way we feel and expect gravity when we throw a ball.

♦♦♦

How to enter
Rice paper room
First
Take off shoes
Yes but my feet
Will leave marks
Then take off feet
How will I walk?
Precisely.

♦♦♦

Rice paper room
You know you want to
Burn it down
How to be and not be
In rice paper room.

♦♦♦

ZEN THINKING

The uninevitability of things is a fundamental of nature.
The fact that things do nearly always happen as predicted
is neither here nor there.

> This spoon
> Is dirty
> This spoon
> Is clean.

Comment:- *this poem is so tight. This poem is a one thousand mile pilgrimage. This poem is sitting on the toilet.*

◆◆◆

> Searching
> For Babylon
> I plant
> A crabapple
> In Babylon.

◆◆◆

Tea Ceremony Suite

Unseen unknown
But understood
The perfection
Of the tea ceremony
Allows freedom.

Mountains collapse
Tea ceremony remains
Perfectly still.

Human bombs make flesh
On spattered walls
A cup is passed
In the tea ceremony.

A rock wren
Flits from
Fir to fir
So
Tea ceremony.

◆◆◆

ZEN THINKING

The purpose of Zen writing is to point, not to make a point.

♦♦♦

Road sweepers
Secretly
Plant crocuses.

Comment:- *Buddha in every action, beauty in intent.*

♦♦♦

Zen offers
The chrysanthemum
Nothing more
Nothing.

Comment:- *this poem is an expression of freedom. It is saying how simple Zen is, how you do not need to be encumbered by icons, rituals, laws, reams of books etc.*
At this point I should explain that it is my position that poems should never be explained but here I express my freedom by having the freedom to contradict myself. All comments are, of course, just that, comments and all poems are open to interpretation. The best (and most) a poem should do is point.

♦♦♦

ZEN THINKING

Contradictions, far from being a stumbling block, in Zen are oddly attractive like chunks in a soup. They are a challenge to the Zen thinker, not to break down, as you might think, but to swallow without choking; in fact, with a little smile – " Look this is perfect and I'll show you how perfect; see here where it is broken".

◆◆◆

The skylark sings
In spite of
The size of
The sky.

◆◆◆

How many great poems did Basho write?
Why none
Did he write any good poems?
Nope!
What about bad poems?
None that I'm aware of.
Well, how many poems *did* he write?
Why none of course.

Comment:- *Basho was a great Japanese poet, allegedly!*

◆◆◆

MOMENTS IN MEDITATION

A poor man queued for soup from the soup kitchen. He then stood outside warming his hands on the bowl. A stray dog, smelling the hot soup, came and sat beside him. The man continued to warm his hands but did not drink the soup. After perhaps fifteen minutes, when the soup had cooled, he set it down and walked away.

Comment:- ...*not looking back.*

❖❖❖

Purity
Wears a white robe
Purity
Does not walk
She floats
Hold her hand
And
She floats away
You know
She'll never
Come back.

Comment:- *embrace purity and it becomes impure.*

❖❖❖

Holding
A rotten apple
I burst into tears
And promptly
Disappear.

Comment:- *purity is invisible, that is to say, everything you see is impure; embrace the impure and it becomes invisible, pure.*

◆◆◆

ZEN THINKING

The flawless mirror is invisible. It is the same for the perfectly enlightened. They become what you see. You see what they become.

◆◆◆

Zen is *the spinner*
After *the quickie*
The batsman
So easily beaten
By the slowness
Of it all

Comment:- *snails on garden walls are dancing.*

❖❖❖

On the bottom
Of my staff
I have cut
A shape of Buddha
So that
With every step
I stamp the world
With Buddha
One step behind
It is wiped out
By Buddha.

❖❖❖

ZEN THINKING

It is only in the perfecting of order that we can come to appreciate and understand disorder.

❖❖❖

Perfect order
Perfect chaos
Tea ceremony or
Chimps tea party
Neither silly – both.

Comment:- *perfection/imperfection, order/disorder, inside the tea hut/outside the tea hut – there is no inside/outside, no either/or, just a spectrum. Disorder is an aspect of order, order is an aspect of disorder, perfection is in imperfection and imperfection is in perfection. One and another are not separate, calm has no existence without storm and storm is pointless without calm, and so;*

Tea ceremony
A storm
In a tea cup.

◆◆◆

ZEN THINKING

It is not so much that things are all the same it is that they are *of* the same and remember most important in the things is to include the self.

◆◆◆

If you think
It is going
To rain
Take an umbrella
In fact, no
Because
It never rains
Unless of course
It is raining.

❖❖❖

Watching
Is waiting
See or
Do not see
Do not watch
Do not
Wear a watch.

❖❖❖

ZEN THINKING

There are only two aspects of Zen poetry; the aspect that points to Zen and the aspect that is *of* Zen. That is to say poems that point the way to Zen in thinking or being and poems that are direct expressions of Zen, both aspects may of course appear in the same poem.

♦♦♦

Zen
Is donut
Shaped

Comment:- *from any point in any direction for ever, no end, no beginning; the torus.*

♦♦♦

Inky black
Silky black
Apple black
Flamingo black
Black black
The singularity
Of darkness
Pointing.

Comment:- *what color is a flamingo in the dark?*

♦♦♦

Sitting on
The stone steps
To the temple
I fall in love
With the stone
Opening up
The metal doors
Of the temple
I fall in love
With the metal
Looking at
The wooden statue
Of Buddha
I fall in love
With the wood.

Comment:- *here is the world, the right way up!*

❖❖❖

ZEN THINKING

Zen, unlike other belief systems, has no fixed point.

❖❖❖

And
In the sea-washed sand
Twisted and torn
Are found the gates
To Avalon

Is it here then
Is this Avalon
Or were these
Twisted members
Washed from
Some distant place
That is forever
Avalon.

Comment:- *'door', 'gate', even 'gateless gate' are all used so much in Zen writing. All imply a wall, hedge or fence; a division. In Zen of course there are no dividing lines because there are no divisions. These words, 'door, gate, gateless gate' can only be used in the sense of their non existence or their breaking down to reveal Zen. In Zen there are no gates or doors to go through. All gates and doors are outside Zen but Zen of course has no outside or inside which leaves gates and doors as mere wooden or metal stand-alone structures, twisted and torn in the sand, important only to themselves.*

♦♦♦

ZEN THINKING

Understanding is a circular thing in Zen. It begins at 0 degrees with no understanding, then proceeds with increasing understanding through another 359 degrees before one more degree takes the student to complete understanding, 360 degrees, which is also 0 degrees, no understanding. The instant of complete understanding is no understanding and no understanding is just being. This is why we say there is no need to understand anything, including this. Understand only this and you will have achieved no understanding.

Comment:- *congratulations! – I think.*

♦♦♦

The diver stands
Perfectly still
Ten toes in a row
Somewhere
An elephant farts
The crowd laughs
The stench is awful
The diver collapses
The pool empties
Everyone leaves
The diver stands up
Ten toes in a row
She is three months
Pregnant.

♦♦♦

I need to explain myself
...uno dos...
To myself in order
...tres cuatro...
To become disordered
...cinco seis...
Dismissed disassembled
...siete ocho...
And then to transcend
...nueve diez...

♦♦♦

ZEN THINKING

I exalt you all to make a stamp, the kind you see on official documents, but make this one in the shape of the Buddha. Then go into the world and stamp things, anything, with his image. You should each choose a different color for your stamp until all the colors and all the shades of the rainbow have been chosen; that way when you stamp you will color-in the world – what do you mean, 'it has already been done!?'

♦♦♦

ZEN THINKING

There is no such thing as disharmony.
Everything is in harmony exactly as it is.
Change your eyes and you will see this is so.

❖❖❖

Wherever you live
Live
In a beautiful place.

❖❖❖

Old fox
Smokes in sly corners
Old fox
Sips wine
From a watering can
Old fox
Sleeps with the hens
He curls
Covers his nose
With his tail
And flattens his ears
Against the horn.

❖❖❖

MOMENTS IN MEDITATION

A monk asked a Zen master,
"What is the great awakening every day?" The old man replied,
"Today I have new socks."

Comment:- *the master's reply says two things: one, the great awakening is mundane and two, it is not a particular thing, it is whatever is on that day (I don't think he had new socks every day!).*

❖❖❖

How to enter perfect void
With all imperfections
Leave them behind?
No take them with you
Sure they make
No difference
None at all.

❖❖❖

Oceans drown
The fishes rise up
And speak
Mountains crumble
The people sit down
And birds walk away
From burning air

The three great realms
Of earth air and water
Are no more
The void the void!
A tiny frog sits
On my wet shoe.

Comment:- *under my weight that shoe will sink into the ground, form a puddle and the puddle a pond. The frog will grow and, one day, jump into the pond just in time for old Basho to come along (oh! do keep up now!).*

❖❖❖

ZEN THINKING

In Zen we struggle to defeat the ego using the ego as our weapon. It is smashing the mirror with the reflection.

> Zen defeats
> Ego with
> The ego
> Breaks
> The glass
> With
> The reflection.

♦♦♦

> Even the perfect mirror
> Cannot see itself
> Only the perfect mirror
> Cannot see itself
> Even the perfect mind
> Cannot see itself
> Only the perfect mind
> Cannot see itself.

Comment:- *encompassing all no viewpoint remains.*

♦♦♦

Pitch black
Empty black
Cellar black
Blackboard black
Inky black
Black black
Black night
A firefly.

❖❖❖

ZEN THINKING

There is an element of disbelief in all of us. We need to cultivate this disbelief, grow it, until it fills our minds. This is not easy, disbelief is uncomfortable, it leaves a hole and we don't like that but it is the only way so,

Believe in disbelief
Have faith in it
Cultivate it grow it
Until it fills
Your field
Then disbelieve
This disbelief
Have faith in it
Cultivate it grow it
Until it fills
Your field
Constantly arising
Disbelief dispels
Constantly arising
Illusion.

♦♦♦

Stone temples
Cannot be seen
By hummingbirds.

Comment:-
Smashing heads
On rocks
The sun
Comes out.

♦♦♦

Down by the river
Fetching water
She is spotted
And she spots
The mountain lion
Has her in his fiery gaze
And she receives him
With her doe eyes
In that moment
She is penetrated
The child is born
Grown and gone
And she withers
And is barren
In that moment
The mountain lion too
Has his peak and is
Old and slow prey
To be spotted
In that moment
Who sees this
Who knows this?

❖❖❖

A flower opens
And
Is dead withered
And gone away
You can see
The one in the other
The other in the one
The one is the other
The other is the one
Not sequential
But simultaneous
Not simultaneous
But the same
All
In one moment.

♦♦♦

ZEN THINKING

Mankind is part of the consciousness, of the thing, the energy, that forms the universe. Our mistake has been to suppose that we are a separate part, a separate consciousness, separated from the energy, we are not; we are just the part of the energy that is able to see itself. When we look at the universe we are not looking at many things but at many manifestations of one thing of which we are just one.

♦♦♦

The part of me
That is still skipping
Not the skipping
With a rope
That children do
But the skipping
Children do do
On the way
To play
That part
That's the part
I have to pick
Like a dead fish
Out of the water
And blow air
Into its gills
Make it live
And grow
And skip
Or swim
Away.

❖❖❖

ZEN THINKING

Thoughts recalled from meditation often make no sense when you begin to practice. This is good and, this is bad; good because on returning to the delusion of everyday life, from this point of view, the simple truth of Zen should make no sense, *ergo* these thoughts are authentic; bad precisely because you have returned to the delusion of everyday life. If and when you do not return Zen begins to make sense.

♦♦♦

Moon through cloud
Morning comes soon
The prairie crocus.

♦♦♦

ZEN THINKING

Knowing all is still we are not confused by motion.

Knowing that time is an invention we have no need for regret or desire.

Knowing that space does not exist we can reach and touch all things.

All things that ever were or shall be, still, at one point.

♦♦♦

Looking the Other Way

Place a banana
In a room
And observe it
Have a banana
Placed in a room
And observe it
From outside
Have an object
You do not know
Placed in a room
And observe it
From Pluto looking
The other way.

Comment:- *is this the plutonium viewpoint?*

♦♦♦

When you enter
A room
You leave
A room
Not entering
You are in
All rooms
This is
The way
Of Zen.

Comment:-*now not entering rice paper room.*

♦♦♦

Sitting in the sun
Hat pulled down
Eyes set
On the horizon
No
No pterodactyls
Today.

Comment:- *no jiggery-pokery just juxtery-pokery.*

♦♦♦

ZEN THINKING

Take all that you know and all that you don't know (which amounts to the same thing) and pass it through the mangle of Zen, not piece by piece but all at once; break all the bones. What comes out is pure; it is just *this*. Alternatively you could pass one thing through the mangle of Zen, look at it, and it and everything else will also become *this*, only *this*.

♦♦♦

If I were
To give
A grain of rice
To the universe
It would be

Too much.

♦♦♦

Other
Same.

♦♦♦

Seven hundred
And fifteen moons
Wash my plate
I am a banana.

Comment:- *a death poem, please adjust the number of moons to fit my age when I die.*

♦♦♦

Being
Not calm
Is part of
Being calm.

♦♦♦

ZEN THINKING

When we talk of our everyday conscious mind, we by definition imply an unconscious; there cannot be one without the other. This unconscious is variously called the great unconscious or the subconscious. Whatever it is called it is effectively defined by the everyday conscious

mind in the negative, i.e. *not* conscious. It is never ascribed any positive attributes. At best the unconscious is seen as an idiot, a simpleton given to simplistic urges and definitely not to be taken seriously. It is not allowed into the playground of the everyday conscious mind.
It is with this idiot, this great unconscious, that meditation sits; this is from where it draws its strength. Meditation draws out the wisdom of the idiot, the simpleton, the great unconscious, and brings it into everyday consciousness and this wisdom is here called Zen.

Slip into meditation
Feel the mighty river
Wash through you
Words now cannot say
Naked in the sun
It is the idiot's way.

♦♦♦

MOMENTS IN MEDITATION

Imagine yourself to be a tree completely aware of your surroundings and completely unaware of your roots. This is the state of the everyday mind and the great unconscious. The everyday mind in all its cleverness is completely oblivious to the role played by the great unconscious in sustaining it. It is the roots which sustain the tree, which are the foundation from which it grows. Put simply Zen takes you to the roots of your existence and resets your mind, from there all flows.

♦♦♦
Bull in a China shop Suite

Was there ever
A bull
In a china shop?
And if there was
Don't you just think
That he tip-toed
Around carefully
And left quietly
By the back door
Perhaps just disturbing
One tea cup
With his tail.

Comment:- *this is an aspirational poem; for bull read ox, the ox of the untamed mind, of The Ten Ox Herding Pictures in Buddhist literature. The tamed ox, as he becomes, stands quietly in the pasture, no whip, no harness needed, he could dance the gig in a china shop and disturb not even the dust and this is the aspiration of the poem. So, why the last three lines? – Perfection in imperfection/ the grain of sand that makes the pearl, I can't explain but it has to be.*

The bull is in the china shop
The plates are smashed
The bull is in the china shop
The plates are not smashed
The bull is not in the china shop
The plates are smashed
The bull is not in the china shop
The plates are not smashed.

Comment:- *the bull of Zen is busy here. He does all of these things and of course there is also no bull and no china shop. So, was there ever a bull in a china shop? – all possibilities arise.*

♦♦♦

ZEN THINKING

Zen is to see without looking.

Zen is to understand without enquiry.

Zen is to acquire without desire.

♦♦♦

Empty mind
Is
Full mind.

ZEN THINKING

Individual existence is like a dancing fountain; jets of water suddenly arise from the reservoir and then just as suddenly return and then arise again. These jets of water represent everyday life, us, all things. The body of water in the fountain, the reservoir, represents the great unconscious. In everyday life we are only aware of the jets of water in the air; we are, if you like, the droplets in those jets, you and me. Everyday life has no awareness of the main body of water, the great unconscious, to which it returns, and must do so, time and time again.

Zen simply provides an understanding of both the water in the air and the reservoir below; the one in the context of the other and the other in the context of the one. The realization of this understanding necessarily ends suffering, ends desire. What you now see is really what you get; come on in the water is…….well….the water.

♦♦♦

Zen points to the moon
Then while we look
Takes our clothes off.

Comment:- *it is not 'what you are doing' but what 'what you are doing' does to you.*

♦♦♦

Open mouthed
In the desert
The lizard.

♦♦♦

The swimming pool
Is empty even though
It has leaves a dead rat
And a flat basketball
We say it is empty because
It has no water
So it is with the mind
In meditation ignore
Leaves dead rats and
Flat basketballs
The swimming pool
Is empty – a frog!

♦♦♦

Being kinder
To stones
And rocks.

♦♦♦

Not where you walk silly!
How you walk
Now enter
Rice paper room.

Comment:- *in life we are taught where to walk; Zen teaches us how to walk.*

♦♦♦

Bert and Harry (finally!)

I thought I'd let these two sometime conversationalists have the last word as they haven't had a chance to say anything in this volume.

H : "What *is* it all about then, this Zen?"
B : "Look, in everyday life we channel the mind, we point it at a problem and shoot and this is how we overcome the obstacles which prevent us from having an easier, more pleasurable, more successful life and that's what modern life is all about right! But this is not the greatest strength of the mind. The greatest strength of the mind is to transcend, to encompass all and realize oneness. This is the strength we must cultivate and we cultivate it through meditation.
It is simple really, in meditation we reach for 'no thought', 'still mind' follows and 'no mind' follows that and after that comes 'Zen mind' ('no mind' with understanding if you like). Only the first stage, reaching for 'no thought' is voluntary, the other stages follow automatically; it is the way of Zen, it is becoming understanding. Here, have a few bullets;

Zen is experiential and it is experienced through meditation.

Meditation itself will take you to the way/path of Zen.

The way/path of Zen has no end it is an end in itself.

Zen teaching/writing can only point to the path it is up to you to follow it.

B : And,

Zen teaching/writing points to the path in four essential ways;

By emphasizing the importance of meditation.

By helping you to learn to meditate.
By knocking you off the rails of conventional thinking thus enabling you to find the path.
By shedding light on the path making it easier to follow.
B : That's about it really, just do it or don't; actually it doesn't really matter whether you do it or not because you already are. It is the realization that counts"
H : "I don't think I understand."
B : "Ah! That's where the Zen comes in, it might be the last bullet; You need Zen to understand Zen."
H : "***##@@!!!"

♦♦♦

AFTERWORD

The journey continues in a series of volumes under the umbrella of 'CONSTANT ARISING' representing, as they do, the ongoing log of a serial meditator following the long and winding path of Zen. The first of these volumes, 'Being Kinder to Stones and Rocks' will shortly be available, an excerpt from this follows after the AUTHOR section.

For more please go to the website
http://www.moonnomoon.com

THE AUTHOR

The author is a mild mannered Englishman, sometime scientist, taxi driver, gardener and artist who now, with his wonderful wife, runs a dog and cat hotel hidden very cleverly in the mountains of Western Canada. Graham has followed the path of Zen for about eighteen years although I'm not sure he knows this. His one wish, through these volumes, so he tells me, is to express Zen, all things being equal.

EXCERPT FROM: BEING KINDER TO STONES AND ROCKS

ZEN THINKING

In winter the problem of snow arises. If I don't look outside in the morning, I get to choose my footwear, if I look, the footwear chooses itself. Whether it is snowing or not depends on whether I look outside. Whether I choose my snow boots or not is dependent, not on whether it is snowing, but on whether I look outside.

Now this might seem like a lot of nonsense but, like a lot of nonsense, it conceals a truth. Let us suppose you can't look outside and you cannot go outside; is it snowing? In a non-evidentiary situation what is evident, what is real? Ultimately we are asking, "What is reality?"

When these sorts of questions are asked Zen is not in the room; Zen is not even next door. Zen is outside, in the snow. You see Zen stands beside this reality, not in front of it. The reality spoken of here is the relative or dualistic reality of everyday thought, Zen reality is of the absolute; in Zen reality it is both snowing and not snowing, boots are worn and not worn; Zen is half way up a mountain potting some geraniums while all this is going on.

❖❖❖

Don't you just love that old teapot with its spout and handle slightly off true. It was probably a second or perhaps it was made before there were firsts and seconds (I wonder, were there ever 'thirds' with no spout or handle – probably not, but how much would we love them!). Anyway, back to the point; why do you love that teapot? That is the question, answering it could take a lifetime.

Comment:-

Constantly arising

The teapot takes form but

Probability makes a boo boo

The handle is off true thankfully

All things are possible and

Frog jumps over moon.

♦♦♦

Made in the USA
Middletown, DE
11 September 2020